LIFE IS MEMORY/ MEMORY IS LIFE

New Poems and Translations by

Gregory Maertz

Finishing Line Press
Georgetown, Kentucky

LIFE IS MEMORY/ MEMORY IS LIFE

To my muse

Copyright © 2026 by Gregory Maertz
ISBN 979-8-89990-326-7 First Edition
All rights reserved under International and Pan-American Copyright Conventions. No part of this book may be reproduced in any manner whatsoever without written permission from the publisher, except in the case of brief quotations embodied in critical articles and reviews.

ACKNOWLEDGMENTS

I am grateful to Finishing Line Press and to my readers for their support.

Along with the canonical poets, music is an important influence on my poetry, most recently the songwriting of River Shook, Jason Lytle, Ilgen Nur Borali, Adam Weiner, Kathleen Edwards, Neko Case, Wes Leavins, Mo Kenney, Orville Peck, Shannon Shaw, Cody Blanchard, Nate Mahan, and Will Sprott.

"The Daughter I Never Had" was first published in *New Jersey Bards Poetry Review 2024: An Anthology of Poetry by New Jersey Poets*, ed. James P. Wagner (Northport, NY: Local Gems Press, 2024), pages 121-122.

Publisher: Leah Huete de Maines
Editor: Christen Kincaid
Cover Art: Gregory Maertz
Author Photo: Lauren Suchenski
Cover Design: Elizabeth Maines McCleavy

Order online: www.finishinglinepress.com
       also available on amazon.com

       Author inquiries and mail orders:
       Finishing Line Press
       PO Box 1626
       Georgetown, Kentucky 40324
       USA

Contents

New Poems

Valley of the Night 1
The Coyote in My Garden 2
Girl with Cornflower Eyes and Raven Hair 3
The Beach on Naxos 10
Wolf's Kiss 11
Falling from Shetland Ponies 12
Eliot House Library 13
The Wine-Dark Sea 14
Arriving in Munich 15
The Daughter I Never Had 16
The Runaway German POW Shot Down in the Woods by an
    American Sentry 17
My First December in Griggstown 18
Griggstown: The Golden Hour in Early March 19
Hunger Stalks the Frozen Land 20
Elegy for a Feral Cat 21
Obsequies for Dying Apple Trees 23
Carpe Diem Poem 24
Our Island Home 25
The Light of Venus on the Surface of Loch Odhairn 26
Gravir on Loch Odhairn 27
Calanish III 28
Hebridean Midsummer's Eve 29
Hebridean Summer Morning 30
Honolulu 31
Kaimana Beach 32
Sonnet: For Amelia Earhart in 2024 33
Lawrence of Arabia 34
The Afterlife 35
Latemar 36

Translations

Standing Rearguard Against the Persians 39
Maui Rodeo Song 41
The White Rose 43
Mignon 44
Suleika 45
To the Moon 46
Bread and Wine 48
Heidelberg 49
The Ballad of Lorelei 50
The Unknown God 51
Nietzsche 52
Come into the Park They Say is Dead 54
The Couple 55
The Prophecy of Our Silence 56
The Blue Dragoons 57
The Morning Devotion 58
The Archaic Torso of Apollo 59
The Panther: in the Jardin des Plantes, Paris 60
Your Voice 61
Embers 62
Autumn Song 63
Epilogue for J. 64
Summer Dreams 65
For A. 66
The Silent Vigil 67

Biographical Note 69

"You cannot step twice into the same river; for fresh waters are ever flowing in upon you."
Heraclitus

"The purpose of literature is to turn blood into ink."
T.S. Eliot

PREFACE

What we call "life" is endlessly in flux, instantly shifting from the future to the past with our bodies serving as the medium of this transition. By the time we have moved, sensed, or observed an event, that experience has already entered the past. Moreover, we cannot avoid living in the past because our consciousness—whether waking or dreaming—is comprised solely of memories. And while these memories are mere shadows projected on the walls of our imagination, they are the most substantial proof that we have weathered life's pageant of glory and trauma. In this new collection of poems, I return to some of the encounters and places—at home and abroad—whose impact on me has been long-lasting. This includes translations—real and imagined—of poems from German, Ancient Greek, and Hawaiian that are as much a part of me as my lived experiences.

Valley of the Night

In the valley of the night
The reddening sky is a succession of tints
From deep arterial black
To the faintest rouge of a superficial nick.

In the valley of the night
Our every breath tastes of blood,
Sour wine, and the coppery scrapings of earth.
Terrestrial creatures are bounding forth
Across the land and flinging themselves into the sky,
And the air is alive with clouds of fireflies
Exhaled by the heaving forest.

Sinking sleepward,
We feel most keenly the return of memories
Of things that we once loved,
Which flutter around our heads,
Homing soundlessly,
With their needle-sharp teeth,
In bat-wheeling, ever-tightening circles,
To our tender-skinned throats.

In the valley of the night,
As embers rise in the eyes of the fire,
The seething ground vibrates
Through the soles of our feet,
And our hearts beat in rhythm
To the soughing of the trees.

The Coyote in My Garden

On a morning before Venus in the eastern sky had set,
Another break of day without you warming my bed,
I encountered a coyote bitch outside my garden shed.

Her fully armed pistol head cocked
Toward the sound of my opening door,
And our apprehensive eyes locked:

Her glance was, like yours, icy and aloof,
Just weeks before Corona bared its teeth
And stole away with our collective breath.

Amber-irised, silver maned, red flanks rippling,
The phantom lurched past me, flickering
Through the lichened rails of the fencing

And athwart the bird bath, giving
Me one last furtive look, before leaping
Over the creek and easefully slipping

Through the cracked door of the shed of rusting
Cider presses where her pups, in full cry, were waiting
For the voles clenched between her lips, quivering.

The sight of this grey wraith just yards away
Shot freezing pulses up and down my spine.
Who posed the larger threat to whom?

I might have given her a similar fright—
Another ravenous predator she might,
For the sake of her young, have to fight.

Girl with Cornflower Eyes and Raven Hair

For L.A.K.

Come back to me,
Girl with cornflower eyes
And raven hair,
Come back with me,
To Paris, during
Our summer there,
To our attic apartment
On the Rue de Grenelle,
Not a stone's throw
From the Musée Maillol—
Living on coffee and kisses,
Sweltering at night in the late May heat,
Surfacing like swimmers to gulp fresh air
From dormer windows flung open.
Falling back asleep with our bodies
Folded together
And your chin cradled
In my arm's crook.

Come back to me,
Girl with cornflower eyes
And raven hair,
Come back with me
To the beach at Sanary-sur-Mer,
During our summer there—
Gorging on Bouillabaisse
We saved for days for,
Eating baguettes and Camembert
At every meal enroute to the South,
Drinking wine cheaper
Than bottled water,
Sleeping on the moist sand
In our sleeping bags,
Waves lapping at our feet.

Come back to me,
Girl with cornflower eyes
And raven hair,
Come back with me,
To the Isle of Naxos, during
Our summer there,
To the white-washed stone cottage
On the goat farm
We rented for a dollar a day—
Listening to the twice daily forays
Of the goats clopping to and from
Their stony grazing pasture,
Drinking retsina at night
In the tiny village of Filóti,
Feasting on walnut-sized peaches
Grown in mountain orchards
And brought earthwards
On a donkey cart.
Come back with me,
Girl with cornflower eyes
And raven hair,
To the plain stone altar
On the summit of Mount Zeus.
We'll make a fresh oblation
To the father of the gods
Of ripe pomegranates
And aromatic thyme
Plucked from the rocky slopes
On our journey towards the sky.

Come back to me,
Girl with cornflower eyes
And raven hair,
Come back with me
To the island of Corfu,
During our summer there—
Diving into the cobalt sea,
Clasping each other
In the burning sand more tightly

Than anyone before or since,
Plunging helmetless,
Astride our Vespa,
Down the narrow strips of road,
From the blue-sky heights
To the bone china beaches.
Reading aloud at night from
The Greek Anthology
And *Zorba the Greek*,
Before falling exhausted
Into a tangle of neither you
Nor me but us.

Come back to me,
Girl with cornflower eyes
And raven hair,
Come back with me
To Athens, during
Our summer there—
Watching a Euripides tragedy
In the Acropolis's Odeon theater
Under a full moon,
Catching your face
By the ears in the dark,
Licking dried grease
From each other's lips,
Smears of the souvlaki
We foraged in the Plaka.

Come back to me,
Girl with cornflower eyes
And raven hair,
Come back with me
To Salzburg, during
Our summer there,
To our private castle turret—
Leaving rose petal stains
On the bedsheets,
Drinking Grüner Veltliner at night

With minor Hapsburg nobles,
Blithely strolling again
In the geometric gardens
And quaint cobbled streets
With marzipan houses that
Echoed with clipping horseshoes.

Come back to me,
Girl with cornflower eyes
And raven hair,
Come back with me
To Rome, during
Our summer there,
To the Forum Romana—
Spilling sacramental wine
In honor of the sleeping gods,
Dodging cassocked guards
In the dark corners
Of St. Peter's Basilica,
Our bare suntanned legs
A sacrilege or a blasphemy,
Paying homage to
Shelley and Keats
Beside the Pyramid of Cestius,
Roaming the streets
On hot Roman nights,
With thirst unquenchable.

Come back to me,
Girl with cornflower eyes
And raven hair,
Come back with me
To the red-tiled domes of Florence,
During our summer there—
Reading Dante and Berenson at night
To the screaming of
Mopeds and motorbikes,
Buying showers
And renting thin, sandpapery towels

For a few lira more,
Washing the road grime
From each other's
Legs and feet,
Shampooing your
Thick black tresses
Under a rivulet
Of lukewarm water,
(I would know the contours of
Your face with eyes closed
And fingers outstretched)
Drinking thin black coffee,
Wolfing down yeasty white rolls,
In the fresh world of morning.
Come back with me
To the shimmering hot days
Inside the perpetual shade
Of Tuscan church walls frescoed
By Piero della Francesca,
After centuries still unrestored.

Come back to me,
Girl with cornflower eyes
And raven hair,
Come back with me,
To Upper Bavaria,
During our summer there—
Giving each other
Matching Beatles haircuts
Without a mirror
Or sharp scissors,
You, a boyish waif
Out of Dickens,
And I, with
All my cowlicks,
Activated by electric shocks.
Weeping inconsolably
After visiting Dachau,
Trying to grasp

The sheer horror of it,
Seeking to reconcile
Species self-hatred
With our raging appetite for life.

Come back to me,
Girl with cornflower eyes
And raven hair,
Come back with me
To the grey chalk towers
Of the Dolomites,
During our summer there,
To the green black
Fore slopes of Latemar
Above the Hotel Bewaller—
Gathering yellow alpine orchids,
Pink rockfoils and Edelweiss,
Torch-shaped indigo gentians,
And deep-hued Tyrolean violets,
Weaving fragrant garlands for your head.
Come back with me
To the wildflower meadows
Of the Eggental,
Riding bareback on
Buckskin-coated
Haflinger colts
In the lavender twilight,
Watering the horses and
Cooling our hot faces
In down rushing
Snow melt streams.
Come back to me,
Girl with cornflower eyes
And raven hair,
Come back with me
Under the shadowing pines
Below the jigsaw ridges of Rosengarten,
Where we devoured fistfuls

Of wild blueberries,
Finding them in
The near darkness
By their sweet, spicy,
Nose-tingling perfume,
Tasting the berries' juice
Again, hours later,
When we found each other's
Purple mouths in the starlight.

The Beach on Naxos

A sunrise swim, a mouthful of brine,
The taste of salt on my tongue,
The itch of dried sweat and
The funk of seaweed on my skin.
The muscle memory of how
We merged in an embrace and
Arched our bodies out of
The sand and into the sun,
A pulsing blitz of euphoria
Followed by blackened vision.

Wolf's Kiss

As my lips were brushed by the wolf's kiss,
I felt my heart's hide burst.
Into her emerald eyes I fell,
Pulling her honeydew hair into a fragrant knot.
A torrent of blood released by her touch
Scorched my fingertips and tear-stained face.

Falling from Shetland Ponies

Perhaps the reason you seem so familiar to me
Is that we were once playmates and rode Shetlands bareback,
Our fists full of mane, clinging to their muscular necks,
Until we slid off and fell into the soft meadow grass.
We then played tag with tame lambs who chased us
Into the barn and up to the refuge of the hayloft.

Eliot House Library

We entered through a secret passageway
That I discovered late one night
On a break from oral exam cramming.

I loved reading there after hours
With only the portraits of Harvard
Worthies as witnesses to my larceny.

After leading you through the tunnel,
We lay down together and defiled
The lush century-old Persian carpeting.

The Wine-Dark Sea

On the wine-dark sea the two of us deployed,
Like the Greeks on their fabled trip to Troy.
Instead of a square-sailed wooden battle scow
With a sun-reflecting brass ramming-prow,

We set out from the bootheel port of Brindisi,
Its streets full of German teens swilling ouzo,
On an overcrowded, diesel-belching ferry.
Because of the fearsome heat down below

We sneaked up to the first-class open deck
And atop our summer sleeping bags we slept,
Exposed to the cooling breeze and its kisses
And the argent, profile-carving moonbeams

That silhouetted your sylph's features in the night
And the jagged outlines of Homer's cherished isles.

Arriving in Munich

Chugging past sunflower fields outside the city limits
On the Intercity from Berlin,
Waiting for my room in the Hotel Blauer Bock
In a cafe on Sebastiensplatz
With an espresso followed by a couple half-liters of Weissbier.
Swiss German tourists speaking English with my Bavarian waiter
Because neither party could fathom the other's dialect.
Walking bikes with baskets full of flowers,
Valkyries taller than midwestern American women pass by.
Talking on cell phones, handsome men dressed
As tastefully as Milanese, seem ready to step onstage.
Whirring past my table on a pink and blue hoverboard,
A pigtailed little girl is followed by her jogging mother.
Somehow this place, after countless visits,
Feels like it could be my Wahlheimat, my chosen home.

The Daughter I Never Had

I see her now and then, most recently
Below Munich's famous clock belfry.
She had the same Kirghiz eyes with

The same arresting blue-grey tint,
The same impish way of placing
Her defiant hands on her hips.

The same luminous, wry,
Fresh apple blossom smile
I would never fail to recognize.

The same born tomboy's disgust
For her blue and white checked
School jumper and collared blouse.

Pushing away a scolding hand
And vehemently objecting to
Her mother's gentle reprimand,

Straddling her pedal bike
And arching her head backwards,
Her snub nose pointing to the sky,

She rolled her blue-grey eyes
And swished her blonde locks like
A wild pony's mane, from side to side.

The Runaway German POW Shot Down in the Woods by an American Sentry

Having escaped the POW cages in Heilbronn,
He was merely trying to get home—
To his family in Handschuhsheim,   *quaint village north of Heidelberg
To his betrothed, Margot, his childhood
  sweetheart.   *my landlady in Heidelberg, 1988

He knew the forested paths
Through the Odenwald from his earliest days.
Reaching the Himmelleiter above the
  castle at night,   *staircase carved into the hillside
He crept through town and down to the river.
He crossed the Neckar rapids in a leaking rowboat with one oar
Before landing on the pebbled northern shore.

He then started hiking up the
  Philosophenweg.   * "Philosophers' Path"
His plan was to reach the deserted and
  derelict Thingstätte   *prehistoric amphitheater
And hole up there for a day or two
Before making a final dash to Margot's house
On the Dossenheimer Landstrasse.

So close to safety, all he sought was to bring an end
To his participation in the nightmare of Hitler's war,
And a bullet through the brain was his reward.

My First December in Griggstown

Scarlet firethorn bushes heavy with berries
Crowd the banks of Cider Creek.
The swaying bird feeders are visited
By overwintering blue jays and mourning doves.

Periods of rain alternate with wet snow.
Awakening to the sound of geese overhead,
While drake and hen mallards are treading water
In shallow pools of overflow from the Millstone River.

Deer graze on woody plants bordering the garden.
They are almost invisible against the grey tree trunks.
Feeling joy again in doing simple chores:
Wheelbarrowing firewood up to the front porch,

Refilling the bird feeders, burning windfall beside
The ancient shed with its moss-covered roof.

Griggstown: The Golden Hour in Early March

In the golden hour before twilight on the cusp of Spring,
A doe and twin fawns enter my back garden.
Daintily they use their lips to browse the oats
Strewn in a white strip across the faded lawn.
As the fawns take their first taste
Their mother nuzzles them by way of encouragement.
Oblivious to their presence, purple house finches forage between their hooves.

Red-winged blackbirds have returned
From their winter migrations
And are joined at the bird feeders
By violet-tinted doves, blue jays, and black-capped chickadees,
Along with a riot of sparrows and dark-eyed juncos on the ground.

A shimmer of ice floats on the D & R canal,
Geese honk in the flooded woods beyond
And from their outposts on the meadow islands in the river.
Still further back, among the willows and drowning ash trees,
Where no one has ventured since the dairy farm closed decades ago,
Wild turkeys repose in their hidden winter colonies.

Like a fidgeting of mice beneath the fallen leaves,
My heart beats out a message beyond the reach of words.

Hunger Stalks the Frozen Land

A cool moon casts its glow
Over the wooded landscape
Like a layer of powdery snow.

Deep pawprints clotted in the slush.
A doe drinks from frigid Cider Creek.
The return of the dark-eyed juncos.

As I drag the carcass of a starved fawn
To the roadside on a tarp, observing me
From a nearby fence post roost, is a hawk.

A squirrel is chased by the vixen
Up the tree beside the bird feeder.
Hunger stalks the frozen land.

Elegy for a Feral Cat

It all began five years ago, when I first put out
A can of cat food, a gratuitous act of kindness,
With no expectation, no inkling of any reward.

I was in a temporary refuge from a bad breakup—
My friend George's magnificent house and garden
In Griggstown on the outskirts of tony Princeton—
When I took pity on a scrawny feral beast:

A black cat with a white daub on his chest,
Doppelgänger to littermates Juju and Jinx,
My dear companions of twenty years,
Whose ashes I had recently strewn there.

Even after moving a mile away
I returned to feed the feral cat every day.
Months of feeding with no contact
One day burst into an affectionate bond.

He had learned to recognize the sound of
My VW and greeted me with his grunting
Little mews, head butts, and loud purring.

Then, this year, starting around Christmas,
The cans of food stopped being eaten.
For weeks I drove up George's driveway,

Hoping against hope that my furry friend
Would trundle down the bluestone steps,
Making his harsh, one-syllable,
Bark-like cries—but he never came again.

And now, in the feral cat's absence—
I am feeling bereft—my sense of loss
Is comparable to the worst hurts I've endured—

Perhaps, the most painful since I was a child,
When I knew no compensating philosophy—
Only raw, searing, heart-stopping grief.

My loss has, however, one consolation:
This tiny creature—his purring, head butts,
And croaking meows so hard won—
Revived my heart and my capacity to mourn.

Let him repose forever in the flowerbeds
Where he often napped, sprinkled with pollen,
In the funerary garden of felines
Who knew the touch of loving human hands.

Obsequies for Dying Apple Trees

Few of them remain that bore witness
To the thriving version of this place,

When the canal thronged with barges loaded
With copper ore from the Sourland Mountains
And coal from the mines of Pennsylvania,
And barrels of hard apple cider earmarked
For the taverns and eateries of New York.

The few that remain are broken and ailing.
Their blossoms fall without yielding any fruit.
But pink and white blossoms they still produce,
Providing nectar for bees and hummingbirds,
And pleasure that reaches deep into my heart.

Carpe Diem Poem

It's high time that we arose,
Threw off sleep's last throes,
Combed our sleep-matted hair
And took a breath of fresh air.

We've lain in bed far too late,
Not heeding the calls of the jays
Signaling that dawn has broken
And our morning chores are undone.

Beneath our feet the floor is cold,
The cat repeats a hungry groan,
Loitering lilac-grey mourning doves
Sit atop the empty birdfeeders, forlorn.

Our little cosmos needs our notice
And yet still we refuse to move.
Cold water is needed on our cheeks,
And clothes suitable for us to be seen.

Then I could rouse the fire in the stove
While you put the much-needed coffee on.
Then the cat and the birds could be fed
And the paper collected from our front step.

Our Island Home

If you bring the matches,
I'll light the candles and
The fire of split oak
And beetle-scarred ash.

If you lay the table,
I'll serve our meal
Of garden produce
Grilled over charcoal.

If you choose the wine,
Red, white, or sparkling,
I'll open the bottle
And fill our crystal.

Beyond our door
The frost on the grass
And the frozen canal

Remind us that our hearth
Is an oasis of warmth
And love is our island home.

The Light of Venus on the Surface of Loch Odhairn

> *"I loved a place of darkness once,*
> *Emptied of people and animals save for*
> *Runaway sheep balancing on the high sea cliffs."*
>   *Scottish Gaelic Song*

The crescent moon rises soon after sunset,
Turning the night into a moon-drenched
Simulacrum of daytime.
The Milky Way emerges later
As if someone had ignited bundled strings
Of Christmas lights with a delayed fuse.
Toward dawn Venus rises
And mimics the light of the setting moon.

On the cusp of twilight, the harsh grunts of herons
Break the silence as they leave
Their fishing grounds on the shore
For their roosts in the noisy heronry
Above the neighboring village called Cromore.
This time they are joined by a recalcitrant chick
With no interest in following its parents homewards.

The surface of the water is as static as glass
And mirrors the mountainous opposite shore
With its collection of houses, ruined and worn,
Acres of blooming Tyrian purple heather, and
Skeins of sheep connected by invisible knitting needles.
Schools of browsing mackerel bubble up
From below as the resident seal is
A swerving torpedo in pursuit.

*Loch Odhairn is a sea loch on the Isle of Lewis

Gravir on Loch Odhairn

     I.

For the first time this summer,
It got dark last night,
But only after the haar* rolled in,   * sea fog
Filling the air with a distillation of salty brine,
The perfume of blooming heather and wildflowers,
With a whiff of peat smoke wafting upwards from my chimney.
The nose was soft and sweet, more Talisker than Laphroaig.

     II.

It was beautifully sunny here today.
I rowed my boat out to the opening of the fjord
And saw a pair of golden eagles, seals, purple-maned jelly fish, and skidding puffins.
It was delightful to drift without purpose and to feel the ocean swell lift the boat,
Rising and falling above the silent, concentrated energy of the sea.

     III.

Just outside my door
The friendly Highland cow gave birth to a calf,
Staining the cow's udder a vivid crimson.
The cow patiently licked afterbirth off the tiny creature.
The calf is the color of caramel.

Calanish III

We plighted our troth inside a forgotten
Stone circle on a remote Scottish island
Where sheep were grazing among
The fallen blue-grey megaliths.

They grazed over the buried bones
Of the nameless ones who worshipped
The sun, the stars, and the moon.
The nameless ones who moved

The massive stones over the sea
To this now empty promontory
Pytheas the Greek called Ultima Thule.
The endless Hebridean rain has worn

Down their faces, but they will endure long
After our mutual enchantment has fled.

*Calanish III is a satellite of the main stone circle of Calanish
on the Isle of Lewis in the Outer Hebrides

Hebridean Midsummer's Eve

With no real darkness on this late June night
The landscape is bathed in redundant moonlight.
Even the foxgloves whose blossoms rise above
The sea of bracken on the northern shore of the loch
Have converted their perfume into luminescence.
And the mayflies, still linked in embrace,
And reluctant to forego any dregs of the sun,
Shoot sparks from their shiny veined wings.

Hebridean Summer Morning

A sunrise of blazing pinks and reds
Gave birth to a warm sun
Hovering just above the horizon.
My friend Martyn's Highland cows
Buck and dance in circles
Around the feed bucket.
The air still carries a trace of
The scent of fresh varnish
On oars resting in the rafters
Of my blackhouse shed.
A mob of unshorn spray-painted sheep
Has sallied from the common grazing
And descended upon the village,
Marauders with designs on my garden.
Raptors orbit high in the angled light.
The grey Eriskay pony leans over the fence
And takes an apple from my hand.
A buzzard mews as it glides
Across my line of vision.
The atmosphere is saturated
With light and humidity as if at
The onset of a tropical storm.
The surface of the great sea loch
Oozes dark chocolate like a lazy river.
Rain is coming soon with a cooling wind.

Honolulu

Driving north on the H-1 highway past Diamond Head,
With the perfume of a hundred flowers in the air,
And the jasmine scent of your breath in my hair,
I ponder what is to be done with my remaining years.

Wild pigs brought here by Tahitians in open canoes
One thousand years ago occupy the green volcanic cliffs
Where they gorge on jungle fruit and succulent roots.
Overhead, the southern stars carve unfamiliar petroglyphs

Upon the face of the liquid alabaster sky that pours
Out of the upturned arms of the crescent moon.
Shall I while away my remaining days and hours,
Toiling, inexorably, in the same paths, well-worn.

Or change my life, as Rilke's famed Apollo,
A mere broken torso, insists that one must do?

Kaimana Beach

Yesterday, when the rain came over Waikiki,
Turning the air into vapor blossoms of gardenia,
And leaving the tennis courts awash in Kalianiole
You were hunkered down in snowy Minnesota,

Thinking it was almost time for bed and
Listening to the mournful howling of coyotes.
As the tide was going out at Kaimana Beach,
Revealing the ragged faces of coral reefs,

You were feeding more wood to the fire,
To keep the embers alive until morning,
And in your head estimating whether
The double-tiered stack was high enough to last

Until winter released its fearsome grip on the
Northern lake country sacred to the Ojibway.

Sonnet: For Amelia Earhart in 2025

The plain bronze plaque on the road below
The crest of Diamond Head is timeworn
But wears a fresh garland of flowers
In remembrance of a bold flight taken

By our lost heroine, who had the courage
To venture what no others had yet done.*
Did Amelia look back with a lump in her throat
And stinging eyes at the emerald Koʻolau horizon?

Did she hear the call of the sounding shore
Even as she launched herself above the clouds?
Daughter of the plains, conqueror of the skies,
Amelia used her fame to defend the oppressed.

How the world needs Amelia and her spirit now
As we lurch back into the throes of darkness.

*Flying nonstop from Oahu to California in 1935

Lawrence of Arabia

> *"I loved you, so I drew the tides of men into my hands*
> *And wrote my will across the sky in stars."*
> T.E. Lawrence, Seven *Pillars of Wisdom*

T.E.'s heart was a house divided
Between his sense of duty to Empire
And his love for a boy, offspring
Of a nation whose fate it was to be betrayed.

Like me, T.E. made promises he could not keep.
We asked too much of ourselves and of so many others.
My soul, like his, is riven by conflicting desires
Whose fate it is to go unreconciled and unallayed.

The Afterlife

Will any of my lovers, friends, and pets
Be waiting for me in the afterlife?
Will my first real girlfriend be there?
What about the last of my great loves?
What about those whose faces
Have faded over the years?

Will I be reunited with the friends
Who moved away in my childhood?
Oh, how we laughed in Cub Scouts
And in our pickup hockey games
On make-shift rinks circled by snowbanks.

What about the friends who died young
For whom I was then too bereft to mourn?
I can still hear my high school tennis partner's
Chirping laughter whenever I try to emulate
His perfect serving motion.

Will Tanga, my pet lioness,
Be waiting for me along with
The menagerie she ruled
With a flick of her tail?

Will I be able to make amends
With the blackbird I killed
With my sling shot
Or the girl I so mercilessly
Teased in the fifth grade?

Will there be flowers, music, and poetry
In the afterlife?
Will my broken heart be mended there?
Will my memories be completely erased
In Lethe's cold embrace?
Or will only the good ones be washed away
To keep me from longing for what I once had loved?

Latemar

       I.   Sebastiensplatz in Munich

A sudden thunderstorm explodes and
A shock of cold air descends on the cobblestones
Of Sebastiensplatz. Echoes of drunken shouts
And clacking footfalls fade as the city falls asleep.
The rain evokes a Riesling aroma from the slate-tiled roofs.

Lay me down in the sea of wildflowers
Below the razor peaks of Latemar. There
The summer song of perpetually airborne swifts
Will comfort me in the austerity of death.

In the morning, I boarded the Austrian train
That runs from Munich to Bolzano
Over the Brenner Pass. The whole way
I anticipated my joy at seeing the Alps again,
One of my young life's most stirring sights.

Different from the thrilling jolt of homecoming
That comes with approaching the sea
Is the vista of mountains. Both evoke awe
And a kind of forbidding, heart-scorching fear,
But only the Alps bring on vertigo.

Leaving Germany over the Danube, whose current is
Charged with whitewater from melting snow,
Whole forests of pine logs are stacked
Onto train cars and glaciers top the grey
Ridge lines like smudges of impasto.

Lay me down in the sea of wildflowers
Below the razor peaks of Latemar. There
The summer song of perpetually airborne swifts
Will comfort me in the austerity of death.

II.   Bewaller in the South Tyrol

The familiar clanging of cowbells in the high meadows.
Haflinger mares grazing beside their pale cream foals.
Apple strudel with springy pastry that resists my fork.
What does it mean to return to this place
Forty years after my first visit?

To wander the same forest paths?
To stand awestruck below the same limestone spires?
To savor the same Austro-Italian food?
To drink the same bone-dry wine?
To hear the same quaintly accented German?

All traces of previous footsteps
On the forest paths have vanished.
All that remains are memories,
Mere ghosts, shadow pictures, less enduring than
Impressions made in the finest grains of sand,
Instantly ephemeral, recorded only in my dreams.

Lay me down in the sea of wildflowers
Below the razor peaks of Latemar. There
The summer song of perpetually airborne swifts
Will comfort me in the austerity of death.

It's a form of active nostalgia, a desire
To merge my present skittering physical self
With the robust joys of youth, to catch a glimpse
Of that glorious time, to taste again
The nectar of new experience, to return
To the arenas in which my lust
For life was first played out.

In the mountains, the passage of time is marked
By the moraine tails of vanishing glaciers and
The spreading shadows of ever soaring pines.
Our lives move along like a speeding train

Over a roaring snow-fed cataract. At any
Moment we might veer off the tracks and
Plunge into the icy tumult below.

Lay me down in the sea of wildflowers
Below the razor peaks of Latemar. There
The summer song of perpetually airborne swifts
Will comfort me in the austerity of death.

Standing Rearguard Against the Persians

An imaginary, so-called "pseudotranslation," of a funerary inscription dating to the Persian occupation of Athens at the time of the Battle of Salamis in 480 BCE. It is written in the first person of a soldier guarding the Greek flanks while the navies of the two adversaries collided just offshore from Salamis, an island west of Athens.

Here I, Arktos, stand behind my shield
With my hoplite's short sharp sword,
Knowing that I will most likely be killed
By a Persian arrow before coming to blows.

But I will nonetheless hold my ground
With my brothers-in-arms, my friends,
Allowing our women, children, and slaves
To escape across the water to Salamis.

Once the Persians have burned the palisade
On the approach to the Acropolis,
They may kidnap my household gods and
They may even desecrate my corpse.

But they won't plunder the Khouroi statues
The lads and I buried in the trenches
We dug behind the wall or smash the marble faces
Of the young heroes fallen in our city's previous wars.

Now the Persians are leaving their
Twin-masted warships on the beach.
They are not coming here to bless
The temple of Athena with wine.

Instead, they bring death, our last friend,
As my comrades and I are fated to die
On this steep, stony ground
Under their showers of piercing darts.

But we shall fall as free men
Defending our fellow citizens.
Free men, who can read and swim,
Unlike those trouser-wearing barbarians.

Alas, there isn't time to free father's rams
From their securely hobbled legs,
Nor is there time to relieve the nannies
Of their milk or comfort their braying kids.

Let the blessed goddess Artemis
See to the fate of our livestock
When I am lying cold on this hill
And my bones are strewn by wolves.

I shall, however, dearly miss
Xanthos, my stout black pony,
As sure-footed as he is keen,
Bred in the mountains of Thessaly.

But we're sure to meet in heaven.
He will wear his silver bridle
And we shall go on endless rides
Over the golden plains of Elysium.

Maui Rodeo Song

A pseudotranslation of a fictional early twentieth-century manuscript written in the Hawaiian language (Olelo Hawai'i) and discovered in the archives of the historic Lahainaluna High School in Lahaina, Maui. Ranching culture was introduced to the Hawaiian Kingdom in the nineteenth century by cowboys from Mexico and South America ("paniolo," Hawaiian for cowboy, is derived from Español). A "charreada," based on Mexican traditions, is a competition combining rodeo along with dressage and other skills associated with expert horsemanship.

Meet me at the old charreada
Down by the Wailua River ford.
We shall watch the white-maned
Palominos and the dappled iron greys
Show off their four true gaits and
Toss their heads with casual grace.

Once there we shall enjoy
Their beauty and easy freedom, too.
We shall take the reins in hand
And dance the way we used to do.

Meet me at the old charreada
Down by the Wailua River ford.
We shall watch the paniolos
From the Big Island drive
Old King Kam's feral cows
To the white sands below.

Once there we will know
Their beauty and easy freedom, too.
We shall take the reins in hand
And dance the way we used to do.

Meet me at the old charreada
Down by the Wailua River ford.
We shall watch the slim Azteca colts
Outpace the big American bays,
While the lean-faced churros vie
With the beef-fed gaucho boys.

Once there we shall know
Why we fled that other place
And why we are splashing
In the turquoise waters now.

The White Rose

A pseudotranslation of a fictional anonymous note found on the memorial to the White Rose anti-Nazi resistance group in Munich's Hofgarten. Following their arrest, the siblings Sophie and Hans Scholl were convicted of high treason in a kangaroo court and beheaded on February 22, 1943.

Who took down your corpses from the guillotine?
Who raised your heads with eyes still glistening?
Was it the executioner dressed in top hat and cravat,
His white gloves stained with your sacrificial blood?

What inspired a dark-haired girl with an intense look,
Who passionately loved poetry, philosophy, and art,
To leave Ulm, her ancient hometown on the Danube,
And confront the monster clawing at the world's heart?

Into the crimson mouth of the wolf she leapt,
Like a conquistador of the human spirit,
Wearing moral armor several sizes too big,
And armed without so much as a toy sword.

Equipped only with their defiant words and bravery,
Leaving the rest of humanity in awe and in shame,
Sophie and her brother Hans dared what few ever do
For the moral values that we so casually betrayed.

Johann Wolfgang von Goethe (1749-1832)

Poet, dramatist, novelist, scientist, and courtier, Goethe is the central figure in the emergence of German literature as a major global influence.

Mignon

Do you know the land where the lemon trees bloom?
The golden oranges smolder in the dark boughs,
A gentle wind blows from the blue sky,
The myrtle stands quiet, and the laurel reaches high,
Do you know it?
There! I would like to go there with you, O my beloved!

Do you know the house and its roof resting on pillars?
The hall glitters, the whole interior shimmers,
And a column of marble statues stands and queries me:
What have they done to you, poor child?
Do you have any idea?
There! I would like to go there with you, O my guardian.

Do you know the mountain and its bridge of clouds?
The mule seeks its way in the fog,
An ancient clan of dragons lives in caves,
First a rockslide and then a flood follows over the cliff:
Do you know this place well?
There! Let's make our way there; O father, let us go!

Suleika

I could never bear to lose you!
Love empowers more loving.
May you grace my youth
With the most powerful passion.
Oh! how flattering it is to my instinct,
If one praises my poet:
Because life is love,
And the life of life is spirit.

To the Moon

Again, you fill grove and valley
Quietly with shining mist,
Which finally also sets
My yearning soul free.

You spread your soothing gaze
Over my landscape
Like the gentle eye of a friend
Contemplating my fate.

Every echo of happy and sad times
Fills my brooding heart,
Between joy and pain, I wander
In sublime loneliness.

Flow on, flow on, beloved river!
Never will I be happy.
Faded away are the love and laughter
As well as the vows of fidelity.

I once possessed it,
That which is so cherished,
That to one's torment
One can never forget it!

Roar, river, through the valley,
Without rest or peace,
Roar, whisper the melody
To my song!

When during winter nights,
You furiously overflow,
Or in the splendor of spring
You help the tender buds grow.

Blissful is he who can retreat
From the world without odium
Keeping a friend close to his bosom,
And with him esteem,

What, unknown or disguised
From the mass of humankind,
Wanders in the dark
Through the labyrinth of the heart.

Friedrich Hölderlin (1770-1843)

Poet and philosopher whose works are famous for combining Hellenic and Romantic themes.

Bread and Wine

Oh no, my friend! We've come too late. Although the gods exist,
They dwell above us in another world.
There they work tirelessly and, while they seem to pay little attention
Whether we live or die, the heavenly ones nonetheless are responsible for our protection.
Because a mortal vessel can only with difficulty contain divinity,
Only at times can humanity endure divine fullness.
Our life is but a dream of the gods. But the madhouse
Helps like slumber and strengthens the longing and the night,
Conditions that nurture heroes in their bronze cradles,
Strengthening hearts that are similar to those of the heavenly ones.
They engage life with thunderbolts. However, it often seems to me
Better to sleep than to live without companions,
So, to wait and to do and say something in isolation.
I don't know, and I wonder what purpose there is in being a poet in a time of cultural poverty?
But poets are, as you say, like the wine god's holy priests,
Who traveled from land to land on the holiest of nights.

Heidelberg

For a long time, I've loved you,
Yearned for you as the object of my desire,
Called you mother and presented you with a clumsy song,
You, the most beautiful city of Germany, as I far as I saw.

As the forest bird flies over the peaks,
Swoops down over the Neckar, where it shines past you,
The bridge is light and strong,
Echoing with the sound of carriages and people.

As if sent by the gods, I am captivated by a spell
That hits me as I am crossing the bridge,
And gazing toward the mountains,
And into the lovely distance,

And the youth, the river, flows toward the plain,
Sadly happy, like the heart when it is too beautiful
For itself to bear, loving to surrender its claims,
Throws itself into the streams of time.

You had refreshment for him, you had cool shadows
To gift the fugitive, and the riverbanks were visible,
Everyone followed him, and from the shuddering
Waves the lovely image of the city arose.

But dominating the valley hung the gigantic,
Fate-anticipating castle, brought down to the ground,
Shattered by lightning strikes.
But the eternal sun poured

Your rejuvenating light over the castle ruins,
Worn down by time, surrounded by flourishing
Green ivy and friendly forests that rushed down
The mountain and enveloped the castle.

Flowering bushes bloom all the way down to the cheerful valley
Where, leaning against the hill or holding the bank,
Your happy streets repose under fragrant gardens.

Heinrich Heine (1797-1856)

Poet, satirist, and political activist whose poems are best known outside Germany in the form of Lieder adapted by the composers Robert Schumann and Franz Schubert.

The Ballad of Lorelei

I have no idea what it implies
That I should feel so sad;
A fairy tale of olden days that
I can't get out of my mind.

The air is cool and it's getting dark,
And calmly flows the River Rhine;
The peak of the mountain sparkles
In the early evening sunshine.

The most beautiful damsel
Is enthroned up there,
Her golden gown dazzles
As she combs her golden hair.

She combs her golden hair with a golden comb
While singing an enchanting song;
A tune that has a supernatural faculty
Inseparable from its haunting melody.

The captain of the small boat
Hears it with intense fright.
He doesn't look at the rocky shoal,
He just looks up into the sky.

I believe that the waves swallowed
The boatman and boat which sank.
And that has to do with the song
The mysterious Lorelei sang.

Friedrich Nietzsche (1844-1900)

Philosopher, composer, poet, and habitual traveler, Nietzsche remains one of the most influential thinkers of his and our time.

The Unknown God

One more time before I move on
And set my sights forward,
I raise my empty hands
Up to you, to whom I appeal,
To whom I, in the deepest depths of my heart
Have ceremoniously consecrated altars,
That always your voice would call me again.

Deeply inscribed on the altar glows
Your name: the unknown god.
I am yours, even if I belonged to the ranks of the wicked
Until the final hour.
I am yours—and I feel the snares,
Which drag me down in battle
And, although I may try to flee,
Force me to serve you.

I want to know you, stranger,
You who reaches deep into my soul,
And enters my life like a wandering storm,
You incomprehensible one, my kinsman!
I want to know you, to serve you myself.

Stefan George (1868-1933)

Mystical poet and object of a cult whose followers included writers, artists, and the leader of the July 1944 German officers' coup attempt against Hitler, George saw the philosopher Friedrich Nietzsche as a prophet of the rebirth of Western civilization.

Nietzsche

Heavy yellow clouds are pulled over the hill,
Bringing cooling storms—half of the autumn offering
And half of the early spring . . . So this mighty fortress
Encastled the Thunderer—who stood apart
From the thousands who emerged out of the dust and
Smoke surrounding him.
Here he sent out over the flat midlands
And the dead city the last dull lightning bolts
And the world went from a longer to the longest night.

Stupidity drags the crowd under—but do not be afraid!
What matters the poisonous sting of sea monsters?
Let's cut down the weeds choking our path!
For a while longer, there will be pious silence
And then the beast will stain you with praise
As you continue to fatten yourself in the darkness.
He who helped strangle you has just died,
Allowing you to stand radiant before the times
While wearing the bloody crown of supreme leadership.

You are the redeemer! Even the most unfortunate
Are burdened with the weight of the lost ones.
Have you never seen the land of the yearning smile?
Did you create gods just to overthrown them?
Are you never to take a rest or to take pleasure in something you created?
You have killed the next god inside yourself
Allowing you to tremble after him with a new desire
And to cry out in the pain of loneliness.

Then the late arriving supplicant pleaded with you:
There is no longer any path over the icy cliffs
And the nests of cruel birds—now it is necessary:
Confine yourself within the circle that is formed by love . . .
And if the austere and tormented voices
Then intone a song of praise in the lilac-tinted night
That forms a bright flood like a lamentation:
The new soul should not speak but sing!

Come into the Park They Say is Dead

Come into the park they say is dead and look around you:
You will see how the shimmer of distant shores—
The clouds of purest white and the sky of unhoped for blue—
Turns the ponds into mirrors and amplifies the colors on the paths.

Once there gather the deepest yellow, the softest grey
From birch trees and boxwood, the wind remains calm.
The late-blooming roses have not wilted entirely yet—
Kiss them for they are exquisite and weave a garland.

Don't forget to pick the last of the asters, too,
The purple flowers wrapped around wild vines,
And, also, what remains of the greenery still clinging to life,
All of which you will gently twist into autumn's face.

Hugo von Hofmannsthal (1874-1929)

Poet, playwright, and opera librettist, Hofmannsthal's lyric poems are admired for their formal perfection.

The Couple

She bore the cup in her hand—
Her mouth formed like its rim—
Her gait was so light and trim,
Not a drop from the cup fell.

He was riding a white mount.
His hand was so light yet firm
That with the most casual touch
He made the horse stand trembling.

But when he leaned down to take
The delicate cup from her hand,
This was so hard for both of them—
They could not stop trembling.

And neither hand the other found,
And dark wine rolled on the ground.

Baldur von Schirach (1907-1974)

Prolific poet and notorious Nazi Party leader found guilty of war crimes at the Nuremberg Trials (1946).

The Prophecy of Our Silence

The sacred silence of all powerful time grows within us—
Serious, steady, and solemn are our ranks.
Then, as the sacred hour wills it, a god
Endows our ardent longing with blessings:
Thus, our prayers are heard, and your desire is sated.
And of your longing, we are also aware.
Deep in your breast you know
Our mouths are speaking of you.

The Blue Dragoons

A folk song popular in Germany from World War One into the Nazi dictatorship.

The blue dragoons, they ride,
Playfully through the gate,
Fanfares accompany them,
Echoing brightly to the hills.

The neighing stallions, they prance,
The birch trees gently sway,
The red flags on the white lances
Flutter in the morning breeze.

Tomorrow, they must ride away,
My beloved will be with them,
Tomorrow, they will ride far away,
Tomorrow, I will be left alone.

The blue dragoons, they ride,
Playfully through the gate,
Fanfares accompany them,
Echoing brightly to the hills.

Richard Dehmel (1863-1920)

Poet of nature and Naturalism, advocate for the rights of industrial workers, and frontline veteran of World War One, Dehmel is considered a master craftsman of poetic form.

Morning Devotion

An old longing roused me early;—
Here where the old oaks murmur,
Lining the edge of the forest,
I yearn to eavesdrop on you, nature.

Trees and bushes seem to have awakened:
All of life pulses on full power,
Reflected in the cool dew that came in the night
The first rays of light tremble with oncoming warmth.

What did you notice first in this profusion of life?
Such all-encompassing greatness! So many little details!
How it fits seamlessly together
Into an all-powerful unity!—

Like the wind rustling in the oats,
The crickets are whirring in the grass all around!
Like a dove cooing in the bushes,
The leaves whisper around his nest!

Like bees hovering about without notice,
The beetles slip quietly through the moss—
Oh nature! what's the point of my stammering
When I see everything interconnected with you?

How it pours into my heart,
All the big things, all the small things,—
How it flows together within me
Into the all-powerful unity!

Rainer Maria Rilke (1875-1926)

Born in Austria, Rilke is considered the most important modernist poet in the German language. The following are translations of "The Archaic Torso of Apollo" and "The Panther," which belong to Rilke's 1907 collection of so-called "Dingegedichte" [thing poems] entitled Neue Gedichte *[New Poems].*

The Archaic Torso of Apollo

We cannot know his magnificent face,
In which his eyeballs shone like ripened grapes.
Yet his torso still glows like a flaming candelabrum,
In which his vision, turned inward, continues to gleam.

Otherwise, the robust contours of his chest
Could not blind you, and the gentle curve
Of his hips could not blend its smile into
The site of all-powerful procreation.

Otherwise, this statue would seem marred,
With arms torn off below the shoulders' transparent ledge,
And it would not continue to shimmer like a predator's fur.
Otherwise, its surface would not burst from all

Its edges like a star: For there is no part of him
that does not see you. You must change your life.

The Panther: in the Jardin des Plantes, Paris

His gaze has, from the endless passing of the cage's bars,
Become so tired that he can no longer concentrate on anything.
It seems to him as if there were a thousand bars
And, behind a thousand bars, no world.

The soft gait of graceful, stronger steps
Which revolves into the smallest of circles,
Is like a dance of strength around a center,
In which there is a great will but paralyzed.

Only sometimes is the curtain over the pupil
Silently raised. Then a picture of the world goes in,
A tense silence passes through his limbs—
And stops in his heart.

Eva Scharfenberg (1915-1987)

The following poems are pseudotranslations of unpublished manuscripts by a fictional Munich-based Art Deco artist and designer. Her once promising career went into eclipse during the anti-Modernist pogroms of the Nazi period. These youthful poems, composed during her years of internal exile, are noteworthy for their emotional intimacy and erotic tension.

Your Voice

For the nonce, the sofa makes
A safe place to lie ensconced
While fending off an ominous future.

Outside, the blustery wind swirls
The dangling windchimes into
Incongruous pieces, and the
Steady downpour batters the
Helpless germaniums.

Rummaging through your old letters,
Your voice comes alive before stinging eyes,
And rends my heart with its indomitable honesty.

Embers

As we sat alone together in
Your apartment I felt the uneasiness
That my presence caused you
And I was suddenly afraid that I'd lost you.

The fire in my eyes crackled and
The embers of love showered and fell
At your feet which you only drew
Further under your crossed legs.

What is there to say?
How is one to feel
When the longing in your eyes
Cannot conceal the needs of your heart
That cry aloud in the dark?

When the doorbell rang
And you got up to answer it
I suddenly felt the terror
Of my own isolation.

When you returned your mood had changed.
The fire in my eyes burned even more
Brightly and it was met
By an acquiescent glow in yours,
And the flames of love did meld.

What is there to say?
How is one to feel
When the happiness in your eyes
Is at last real and the needs of your heart
Are at last answered in the dark?

Autumn Song

I know that winter is coming
Since the flavor of the wind
Has changed from all the tastes
That I knew at the dawn of Spring.

The infinite disappointment
As the fervid joys of summer
Are remembered, adding sting
To the tears of October's frost.

Although a full cycle of seasons
Has passed since I last held your hand,
Your beckoning glances even now
Send pangs of temptation through my heart.

Epilogue for J.

When you find time
Revive me from the ennui
That plagues my days.

When you find time
We will explore what remains
O the human spirit,

To see what lies inside
Our minds besides
Conditioned responses.

When you find time
We'll share the dreams our
Lives still hold in store.

But I know that your star will not fall
Whereas mine is destined
To reverberate endlessly in the Zodiac.

Summer Dreams

Your radiant smile rides
The crest of every wave,
Falling from water skis, I ply
Your depth with ardent strokes.

Immersed in you, exhilarated by your touch,
Generations of lovers frolic before my eyes
In the sketchy outlines of moonlight.

The halcyon days of discovering you—
Lips, eyes, and hands; skin sleek and
Glistening in the glare of a languid sun.

Intercourse between the seasons,
Lovemaking among the cattails,
Communion in the sandy shoals,
Revelation in a summer's day.

For A.

I love to lay my head in your lap
And watch your hair in cascades
Upon my face.

Each time you brush
The longest hairs dangle in my nose
And cover my lips,
A subtle attempt at suffocation
That'd be better accomplished
Using your delicate fingers
That seem only gently to trace
The curves of my cheekbones
And the hollows of my chest
Where you bury your head
After we've made love.

Each time you breathe
The longest hairs, curly and brown,
Find their way inside your nose,
A subtle attempt at tickling you
That'd better be accomplished
Using my awkward fingers
That seem only gently to caress
Your breasts and the dimples
At the base of your spine.

The Silent Vigil

The silent vigil . . .
Broken by interlopers traversing life
And the oblivion of death,
To catch the final flicker
Of recognition in the eyes
Of a face worshipped in every dream
And caressed in every moment of privacy.

His suffering intensifies . . .
Untold tales of pain and longing
Are revealed in callused hands
And a bruised heart,
The wrinkles etched around his eyes
And mouth convey a far more
Eloquent plea than his vague
Mutterings about immortality.

Her loneliness increases . . .
Frustration in the search for companionship
Revealed in blood-stained eyes gone dry,
The years of canine loyalty are
Finally rewarded by death's release.

BIOGRAPHICAL NOTE

Gregory Maertz is a professor of English at St. John's University in New York City. Educated at Northwestern, Harvard, and the University of Heidelberg, he developed expertise in British and German nineteenth-century poetry, philosophy, and prose fiction as well as German visual art from the 1920s through the 1950s.

A deep immersion in the German language and culture has been central to Maertz's academic career, resulting in the publication of several books and many articles. Maertz has also lent a hand in organizing major international art exhibitions around the controversial theme of cultural production in Nazi Germany. The decision to begin translating classic German poems—by Goethe, Rilke, Hofmannsthal, and others—was inspired by a desire to return to the literary enthusiasms of his youth. The inclusion here of fictional pseudotranslations from imagined German, Ancient Greek, and Hawaiian sources represents an experiment in literary and historical speculation.

Maertz's new collection was written at his home in Griggstown, New Jersey following return visits to Honolulu, the Isle of Lewis in the Outer Hebrides, Cambridge, Massachusetts, the village of Obereggen in the South Tyrol, and Munich. Others were inspired by his travels throughout Europe and a long residency in Heidelberg during his student days. Formally in dialogue with traditional poetic genres like the sonnet and the ballad, Maertz's new poems adapt these forms to commemorate deeply personal experiences and feelings.

Maertz's first book of poems, *The Charisma of Animals* (2023), may be purchased from Finishinglinepress.com and his other books are available on his Amazon author's page.

www.ingramcontent.com/pod-product-compliance
Lightning Source LLC
Chambersburg PA
CBHW030057170426
43197CB00010B/1559